First published in the United States 1984
by Dial Books for Young Readers
A Division of E. P. Dutton, Inc.
2 Park Avenue
New York, New York 10016
Published in Great Britain by Walker Books Ltd.
Copyright © 1984 by Helen Oxenbury

First Edition
(US)
10 9 8 7 6 5 4 3 2 1

Library of Congress Cataloging in Publication Data

Oxenbury, Helen | Our dog

(Out-and-About books)
Summary: A small boy and his mother try to cope with a dog
that loves to go for walks, jump into dirty water, and roll in mud.
[1. Dogs—Fiction.]
I. Title.
PZ7.0975Ou 1984   [E]   84-5829
ISBN 0-8037-0127-6

Our Dog

by Helen Oxenbury

Dial Books for Young Readers

E. P. Dutton, Inc. New York

Our dog has to go for a walk every day.
She stares at us until we take her.

One day she found a swamp.
She jumped into the dirty water.
"Yuck! You smell disgusting!"
we told her.

Then she rolled in the mud.
"Pretend she's not ours,"
whispered Mom.

We made her wait
outside the kitchen door.
Mom filled the washtub.
"I'll put her in," Mom said.
"Now hold on tight!
Don't let her jump out!"

"Quick! Where's the towel?"
Mom shouted. "She'll get
everything wet!"

"Come here. Sit. Stay!" I said.
"I'll catch her," said Mom.

She ran up the stairs and
into the bedroom.
We caught her on the bed.
"It's no use!" Mom said. "We'll just
have to take her for another walk
and let her dry in the air."

So we did!